# *GOLDEN STEPS TOWARDS FINANCIAL FREEDOM*

 GOLDEN STEPS TOWARDS FINANCIAL FREEDOM

# INDEX

We started

The way we think

What we do in our lives

Playing the game to win or lose

# We started

Thoughts lead to feelings, feelings lead to activities, and activities lead to results. It all starts with your thoughts, which are produced by your brain. Isn't it amazing that our brain is practically the foundation of our lives and yet most of us have no idea how this powerful device works? So let's start by taking a simple look at how your brain works.

Metaphorically, your mind is nothing more than a huge filing cabinet, similar to what you would find in your office or home. All the data that comes in is labeled and filed in folders so that it is easy to retrieve it to help you survive.

Did you hear that? I didn't say to thrive, I said to survive.

In every situation, you go to the files in your brain to determine how to react. Let's say, for example, you're considering a financial opportunity. You automatically go to your file labeled as cash and from there you decide what to do. The only thoughts you may have about cash will be those stored in your cash file. That's all you can think about, because that's all that's in your brain under that category.

Let's take a look at how to use these files correctly.

Secrets of the subconscious mind of a millionaire.....how to transfer your financial plan to create unlimited wealth on autopilot in the Internet age.

GOLDEN STEPS TOWARDS FINANCIAL FREEDOM

# The way we think

You decide based on what you feel is logical, judicious and appropriate for you at the time. You make what you feel is the right choice. The point, however, is that your right choice may not be a successful one. In fact, what makes perfect sense for you could consistently produce completely poor results. For example, let's say I'm at the mall. I see this green bag on sale at a 25 percent discount. I immediately go to my brain files with the question "Should I get this bag?" In a nanosecond, my brain files come back with the answer: "You've been looking for a green bag to go with those green shoes you bought last week. Buy it!" As I run to the checkout, my brain not only gets excited about having this beautiful bag, but it shines with pride because it's 25% off.

To my brain, this purchase makes a lot of sense. However, at no point did my brain think to itself "It's true, this is a really nice bag, and it's true, it's a good deal, but today I'm $3000 in debt, so I better wait". I didn't come up with that data because no file in my brain contains it. The "When in debt, don't buy anymore" file was never established and doesn't exist, which means that the specific choice is not an option.

Do you understand me?

**Our brains**

If you have files in your cabinet that are not

supportive of financial success, those will be the only decisions you can make. They will be instinctive, automatic and will make a lot of sense to you. But, ultimately, they will still produce financial failure or mediocrity at best.

Conversely, if you have brain files that support financial success, you will naturally and automatically come up with the choices that produce success. You won't have to consider it. Your normal way of thinking will result in success, somewhat like Donald Trump. Your normal way of thinking produces wealth.

When it comes to cash, wouldn't it be amazing if you could think inherently about how rich people think? Well, you can! The movement of openness to any change is consciousness, which means that the movement of openness to thinking the way rich individuals think is knowing how rich individuals think.

Rich individuals think very differently from poor and middle class individuals. They think differently about money, about wealth, about themselves, about others, and about every other aspect of life. We will examine some of these differences and, as part of your refurbishment, install alternative "wealth files" in your brain.

With fresh files come new options. You may surprise yourself when you are thinking like poor and middle class individuals and consciously shift your focus to how rich individuals think. Remember, you may decide to think in ways that support your happiness and success rather than in ways that don't.

Some precautions to start with. In no way, shape or form do I want to degrade poor individuals. I don't think rich individuals are better than poor ones. They're just richer. At the same time, I want to make sure they get the message, so I'm going to make the distinctions between rich and poor as extreme as possible.

When I talk about rich, poor, and middle-class individuals, I'm talking about their thinking, how different people think and act instead of the amount of money they have or their value to society.

I'm going to generalize. Again, my goal is to

make sure you understand the point of every principle and use it. In general, I won't always refer to the middle class specifically, because middle class individuals commonly have a mixture of rich and poor mentalities.

Several of the precepts might seem to deal more with habits and activities than with ways of thinking. Our activities come from our feelings, which come from our thoughts. Therefore, all rich activity is preceded by a rich way of thinking.

Finally, I will ask you to be willing to give up being right! What I mean by this is that you should be willing to give up having to do it your way. Why?

Because your way has given you precisely

what you have today. If you want more of the same, keep doing it your way. However, if you are not yet rich, perhaps it is time to consider another way. It's up to you. The concepts you are about to learn are simple but profound.

They make real changes for real individuals in real life. If you learn them and use them, I am sure they will transform your life as well.

At the end of each section, you will find a proclamation and a physical movement to "anchor" it in your body. In the same way, you will find activities that will help you acquire this archive of wealth. It is crucial that you put each file into action in your life as quickly as possible so that knowledge can move on a physical, cellular level and produce lasting and permanent change.

Most individuals understand that we are creatures of habit, but what they do not recognize is that there are actually two kinds of habits: habits of doing and habits of not doing. Everything you're not doing right now, you're doing with a habit of not doing.

The only way to alter these habits of not doing into habits of doing is to do them. Studying will help you, but it's a whole different world when you go from studying to doing. If you're really serious about success, try it out and do the suggested activities.

# What we do in our lives

If you want to produce wealth, it is crucial that you are confident that you are in control of your life, particularly your financial life. If you don't trust this, then you must inherently trust that you have little or no control over your life, and therefore have little or no control over your financial success. That is not an attitude of wealth.

Have you ever noticed that it is commonly poor individuals who spend a fortune playing the lottery? They actually trust that their wealth is going to come from someone picking their name out of a hat. Sure, everyone wants to win the lottery, and even rich individuals play for fun from time to time. But first, they don't spend half their salary on tickets, and second, winning the lottery is not their main "plan" for producing wealth.

You have to trust that you are the one who produces your success, that you are the one who produces your mediocrity, and that you are the one who produces your struggle around money and success. Consciously or unconsciously, you are still you. Instead of taking responsibility for what is happening in their lives, poor individuals choose to play the role of victim. The predominant thinking of a victim is often "poor me. So presto, under the law of intent, that is literally what victims get: they become "poor.

Note that I said that they play the role of the victim. I didn't say they were victims. I don't think anyone is a victim. I think individuals play the role of victim because they believe it gives them something.

What we get

How can you tell when individuals are playing the victim? They leave three obvious clues.

**Track 1: Failure**

When it comes to why they are not rich, most victims are professionals in the "blame game". The object of this game is to see how many individuals and conditions you can point to without ever seeing yourself. At least it's fun for the victims. Unfortunately, it's not as much fun for anyone else who is unlucky enough to be around them. That's because those who are close to the victims become easy targets.

Victims blame the economic system, the government, the stock market, their stockbroker, their type of business, their employer, their employees, their manager, the home office, their upline or downline, customer service, the shipping department, their partner, their co-worker, the higher power, and naturally they always blame their parents.

It is always someone else or something else who is to blame. The problem is anything or anyone but them.

## Track 2: Rationalize

If the victims are not guilty, you will often find them rationalizing their situation by saying something like "Money is not really significant. Let me ask you this question: If you were to say that your partner, or your boyfriend, or your partner or your friend, is not that important, would any of them be there for long? I don't think so, and neither would money!

Would you have a motorcycle if it wasn't important to you? Of course not. Would you have a pet if it wasn't important to you? Of course I wouldn't. In the same way, if you don't think money is important, you won't have any.

You may dazzle your acquaintances with this insight. Imagine you're in a conversation with an acquaintance who tells you, "Money is not important. Put your hand on your forehead and look up as if you were receiving a message from heaven, then shout, "You're broke!" To which your scandalized acquaintance will no doubt reply: "How did you know?" Then you hold out your hand and say: "What else do you want to know? That's 50 dollars, please!" Let me put it plainly: Anyone who says cash is not significant has none!

Rich individuals understand the importance of cash and the place it has in our society. On the other hand, poor individuals validate their financial clumsiness by using irrelevant comparisons. They will argue, "Well, cash is not as significant as love. Now, is that comparison dense or what? Which is more

crucial, your arm or your leg? Maybe they're both significant.

Listen, my friends: money is extremely significant in the areas it works, and exceedingly insignificant in the areas it does not. And while love can make the world go round, it certainly doesn't pay for the construction of any hospital, church or house. Nor does it feed anyone. No rich individual believes that money is not meaningful.

**Track 3: Whining**

Whining is the worst thing you can do for your health or your wealth. The worst! Why? I'm a great believer in the universal law that says, "What centers you expands."

When you are whining, what are you focusing on, what is right or wrong in your life? Obviously you are focusing on what is wrong, and as what you focus on expands, you will continue to acquire more of what is wrong. Many teachers in the field of personal development discuss the Law of Attraction. It says that "what is equal attracts what is equal," which means that when you are whining, you are actually attracting "junk" into your life.

Have you ever noticed that whiners often have a bad life? It seems like everything that could go wrong fails them. They say, "Of course I complain, look how bad my life is." And now that you know better, you can explain to them, "No, it's because you complain that your life is so lousy. Shut up...

and don't stand next to me!"

Which brings us to a different point. You have to make sure you don't get in the vicinity of the complainers. If you have to be near them, make sure you carry a steel umbrella or the shit that's meant for them will get you too!

Here are some preparations that I promise will alter your life. For the next 7 days, I dare you not to complain at all. Not only out loud, but in your head as well. But you have to do it for the whole 7 days. How's that? Because for the first few days, you may still have some "residual garbage" coming in from before. Unfortunately, garbage doesn't travel at the speed of light, you know, it travels at the speed of garbage, so it can take a while to clean up.

Failure, rationalization and whining are like pills. They're just stress reducers. They relieve the stress of failure. Consider it. If an individual was not failing in some way, shape or form, would they have to fail, rationalize or whine? The obvious answer is no.

From now on, when you hear yourself failing, rationalizing or complaining disastrously, stop doing so immediately. Remind yourself that you are producing your life and that at every moment you will be attracting success or shit to your life. It is crucial that you choose your thoughts and words wisely!

Now you are ready to hear one of the

greatest secrets in the world. Are you ready? Read this carefully: there is no such thing as a truly rich victim! Do you understand? Besides, who would listen? "Whaa, I have a scratch on my yacht." To which almost everyone would reply, "Who cares?"

What do individuals get out of being a victim? The answer is attention. Believe me; it's almost impossible to be truly happy and successful when you're perpetually seeking attention. Because if it's attention you want, you're at the mercy of other people.

You often end up as a "people pleaser" begging for approval. Seeking attention is also a problem, since individuals tend to do stupid things to get it.

Now, as I said, there's no such thing as a rich victim. So to remain a victim, attention seekers make sure they never get rich. It's time to choose. You can be a victim or you can be rich, but you can't be both.

Listen up. Every time, and I mean every time you blame, rationalize or complain, you're cutting your financial throat. It's time to take back your power and recognize that you produce everything in your life and everything not in it. Recognize that you produce your wealth, your non-wealth, and every level in between.

Proclamation: Put your hand on your heart and say...

"I produce the precise level of my financial

success!"

Touch your head and declare...

"I have a millionaire's mind!"

Every time you catch yourself failing, rationalizing or whining, slide your index finger across your neck, like a trigger, to indicate to yourself that you are cutting your financial throat. Although this gesture may seem a little crude to make to yourself, it is no cruder than what you do to yourself when you blame, rationalize or complain, and it will eventually work to alleviate these destructive habits.

Make a "report. At the end of each day, write

down one thing that went well and one thing that didn't. Then write down the answer to the question that accompanies the question: "How did I produce each of these situations?" If other people were involved, ask: "What was my part in producing each of these situations? This simulation will hold you accountable for your life and make you aware of the techniques that work and those that don't.

# Playing the game to win or lose

Poor individuals play the cash game on defense instead of offense. Let me ask you: If you played any sport or any game purely on defense, what are the chances that you would succeed in that game? Most individuals would agree, few and far between. However, this is precisely how most individuals play the money game. Their main concern is survival and security rather than producing wealth and abundance.

So what is their goal? What is their objective? What is their true intention? The goal of truly wealthy individuals is to have monumental wealth and abundance. Not just some money, but a lot of money. So what is the great goal of poor individuals? "To have enough to pay the bills... and in time would be a miracle!" Let me tell you about the power of intention. When your intention is to have enough to pay the bills, that is precisely what you are going to acquire, enough to pay the bills and not a penny more.

Middle class individuals at least go one step further... too bad it's a dwarf's step. Their great goal in life is also their favorite word in the world. They simply want to be "comfortable". I hate to break the news to you, but there's a big difference between being comfortable and being rich.

## Achievements

I have to admit I didn't always recognize that. But one of the reasons I am confident that I have the right to write this book is that I have had the experience of being on all three sides of the proverbial fence. I've been super broke, like when I had to borrow a dollar for gas in my car. But let me qualify that.

First of all, it wasn't my car. Second, that dollar came in the form of four quarters. Do you know how embarrassing it is for an adult to pay for gas with four quarters?

The boy at the gas pump looked at me as if I was some sort of vending machine thief and then just shook his head and laughed. I don't know if you can relate, but it was definitely one of my financial lows and unfortunately only one of them.

Once I got organized, I graduated to the level of being comfortable. Comfortable is nice. At least you go to decent restaurants for a change. But pretty much all I could order was chicken. There's nothing wrong with chicken, if that's what you really want. But often it's not.

In fact, people who are only comfortable financially often decide what to eat by looking at the right side of the menu, the price side. "What would you like for dinner tonight, dear?" "I'll take this $8 plate. Let's see what it is. Surprise, it's the chicken," for the 19th time this week!

When you're comfortable, you don't dare let your eyes see the bottom of the menu, because if you did, you might find the most forbidden words in the middle-class dictionary: market value! And even if you are curious, you will never wonder what the real price is. First of all, since you know you can't afford it.

Second, it's frankly embarrassing once you know the waiter doesn't believe you when you tell him the dish is $46 with extra sides and you declare, "You know what, somehow I have a real craving for chicken tonight.

I have to say that for me personally, one of the best things about being rich is not having to see prices on the menu any longer. I eat precisely what I want to eat, regardless of the price. I can assure you that I didn't when I was broke or comfortable.

It all comes down to this: If your goal is to be comfortable, chances are you will never get rich. But if your goal is to be rich, you will most likely end up very comfortable.

Among the principles I teach is "If you shoot at the stars, you'll hit the moon anyway. Poor people don't even shoot at the roof of their house, and then wonder why they don't succeed. Well, they just learned.

You get what you really want to get. If you want to get rich, your goal has to be rich. Not having enough to pay the bills, and not just having enough to be comfortable. Wealth means wealth!

**Proclamation**: Put your hand on your heart and your state...

"It is my destiny to become a millionaire and more!"

Touch your head and declare...

"I have a millionaire's mind!"

1. Set two financial goals that demonstrate your intention to produce abundance, not mediocrity or poverty. 2. Write down the "play to win" goals for your:

a. Annual income

b. Net value

Make these goals achievable with an honest time frame, but at the same time remember to "shoot for the stars.

2. Go to a fancy restaurant and order a meal at "market value" without asking how much it costs. (If finances are tight, sharing is acceptable.) No chicken!

## GO AHEAD!! GO FOR YOUR FINANCIAL FREEDOM!!!

Visit our author page on Amazon and get more MENTES LIBRES!

http://amazon.com/author/menteslibres

If you wish, you can leave a comment on this book by clicking on the following link so that we can continue to grow! Thank you very much for your purchase!

https://www.amazon.com/dp/B0836GV3ZZ

www.ingramcontent.com/pod-product-compliance
Lightning Source LLC
Chambersburg PA
CBHW070843220526
45466CB00002B/868